INSECTS

Words that look like **this** can be found in the glossary on page 24.

WHAT IS AN INSECT?

There are so many animals in the world that we split them into different **categories**. This helps us tell all of the animals apart.

One of these categories is insects.

INSECTS

PARTS OF AN ANIMAL

Written by Emilie Dufresne

BookLife
PUBLISHING

©2018
Book Life
King's Lynn
Norfolk PE30 4LS

ISBN: 978-1-78637-433-2

Written by:
Emilie Dufresne

Edited by:
Kirsty Holmes

Designed by:
Amy Li

A catalogue record for this book is available from the British Library.

All facts, statistics, web addresses and URLs in this book were verified as valid and accurate at time of writing. No responsibility for any changes to external websites or references can be accepted by either the author or publisher.

Insects That Fly

Insects That Jump

Arachnids

Insects are one of the largest groups of animals on
this planet. There are lots of different types of insects.

HOW DO YOU KNOW?

We can ask certain questions to find out if an animal is an insect or not.

How do we know that

this is an insect?

6

CHECKLIST

Does it have six or eight legs?

Does it have antennae or feelers?

Does it have two or three separate body parts?

IT'S AN INSECT!

HEADS AND SHOULDERS

Insects look very different to humans, and have very different bodies. Most insects have three body parts, and arachnids only have two.

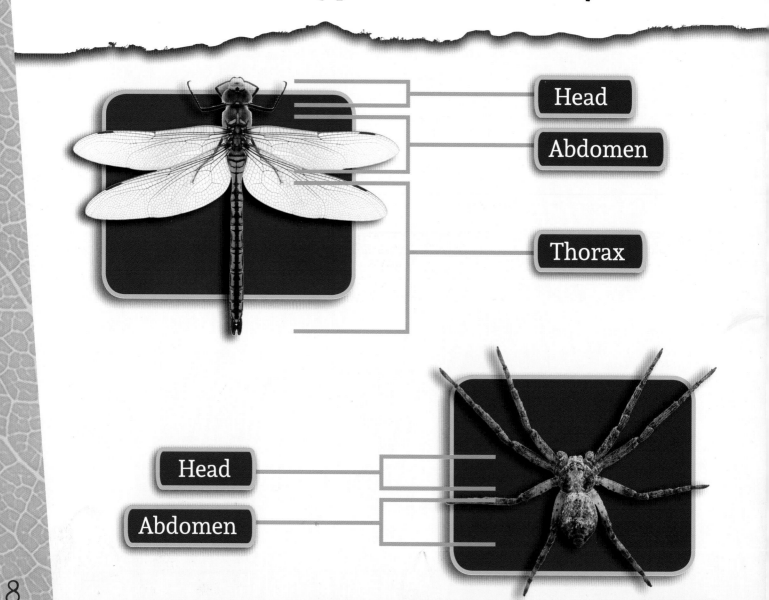

Head

Abdomen

Thorax

Head

Abdomen

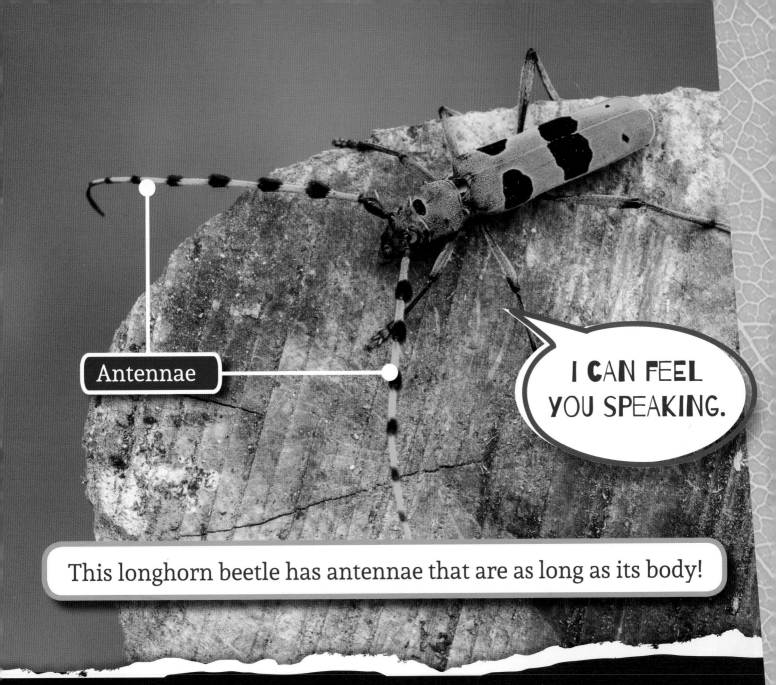

Antennae

I CAN FEEL YOU SPEAKING.

This longhorn beetle has antennae that are as long as its body!

Most insects have antennae on their heads. Antennae are

KNEES AND TOES

Insects don't have knees like humans, but they do have joints that connect different parts of their legs.

All these tiny hairs help the spider stick to the wall.

Have you ever wondered how spiders can climb on walls and ceilings? They have lots of hairs on their feet, which are covered in even more hairs.

EYES AND EARS

Most insects have compound eyes. This means they have lots of little eyes instead of just one. They can't focus like we can, so they see very blurry images.

Fly Eye

This is what a fly sees.

Even though they can't focus, they

can almost see all around them.

Insects don't have ears like humans. Instead, insects hear by feeling sound **vibrations**. This cricket hears through its front

MOUTH AND NOSE

Some insects use their antennae to smell things. Different insects have different mouths depending on what they eat. Some chew, some **siphon** (say si-fon), and some pierce.

This earwig crushes its food using **mandibles**.

Mandibles

Tongue

A butterfly is a type of siphoning insect. Their tongues are straw-shaped, so they can drink **nectar**.

SKIN

Instead of having their skeleton on the inside (like humans), insects have it on the outside. This is called an exoskeleton.

Exoskeletons form in different sections

so that insects can move.

Lots of insects shed their exoskeletons to allow them to grow. Cicadas are a type of insect. They are called nymphs before they become fully grown.

INSECTS THAT BREAK THE RULES

Scorpions are part of the insect family, and are a distant relative of spiders. However, they don't have any antennae.

Instead they have pincers and

a stinger on their tail.

The praying mantis is an insect that breaks all the dinner rules – it eats members of its own **species**!

INGENIOUS INSECTS

Exploding ants give up their lives to save their **colony**. If they are being attacked they blow up their abdomens onto their opponents.

They ooze yellow goo that sticks to the enemy.

Abdomen

This bug doesn't just eat its prey; it injects them with a **venomous** liquid that turns their insides to mush. Then it slurps them up

FUN FACTS

Dragonflies have been on the earth for 300 million years.

Dung beetles don't only roll poo, they eat it!

The average worker bee only makes ½ a teaspoon of honey in its lifetime.

QUICK QUIZ

1. How many parts does an insect's body have?

2. Where is an insect's skeleton?

3. What do spiders use to climb up walls?

4. What do most insects use to sense things?

GLOSSARY

ARACHNIDS	a type of minibeast that has eight legs, such as a spider
CATEGORIES	different sections within a larger group
COLONY	a large group of animals or plants that live and work together
MANDIBLES	the parts of the jaw bone
NECTAR	a sweet liquid made by flowers in order to attract insects
SENSORY	relating to different types of senses
SIPHON	to move liquid by sucking
SPECIES	group of very similar animals or plants that are capable of producing young together
VENOMOUS	capable of injecting venom through a bite or a sting
VIBRATIONS	small, shaking movements

INDEX

24